YOUR KNOWLEDGE HAS VALUE

- We will publish your bachelor's and master's thesis, essays and papers

- Your own eBook and book - sold worldwide in all relevant shops

- Earn money with each sale

Upload your text at www.GRIN.com and publish for free

Bibliographic information published by the German National Library:

The German National Library lists this publication in the National Bibliography; detailed bibliographic data are available on the Internet at http://dnb.dnb.de .

Imprint:

Copyright © 2015 GRIN Verlag, Open Publishing GmbH
Print and binding: Books on Demand GmbH, Norderstedt Germany
ISBN: 9783668271104

This book at GRIN:

http://www.grin.com/en/e-book/336348/autonomic-approach-for-fault-tolerance-using-scaling-replication-and-monitoring

Ashima Garg, Sachin Bagga

Autonomic approach for fault tolerance using scaling, replication and monitoring of servers in cloud computing

GRIN Publishing

GRIN - Your knowledge has value

Since its foundation in 1998, GRIN has specialized in publishing academic texts by students, college teachers and other academics as e-book and printed book. The website www.grin.com is an ideal platform for presenting term papers, final papers, scientific essays, dissertations and specialist books.

Visit us on the internet:

http://www.grin.com/

http://www.facebook.com/grincom

http://www.twitter.com/grin_com

ACKNOWLEDGMENT

DEDICATED TO ALL THOSE PEOPLE
WHO CHANGES THE LIVE OF OTHERS
BY GIVING AS AN EXAMPLE AND BY
EMPOWERING OTHERS FOR GREATNESS

THANK YOU.

HAVE YOU EMPOWERED SOMEBODY
FOR ABSOLUTE GREATNESS TODAY?

ABSTRACT

Cloud based systems are more popular in today's world but fault tolerance in cloud is a gigantic challenge, as it affects the reliability and availability for the end users. A number of tools have been deployed to minimize the impact of faults. A fault tolerable system ensures to perform continuous operation and produce correct results even after the failure of components up to some extent. More over huge amount of data in the cloud cannot monitor manually by the administrator. Automated tools, dynamic deploying of more servers are the basic requirements of the today's cloud system in order to handle unexpected traffic spikes in the network. This proposed work introduces an autonomic prospective on managing the fault tolerance which ensure scalability, reliability and availability. HAProxy has been used to provide scaling to the web servers for load balancing in proactive manner. It also monitors the web servers for fault prevention at the user level. Our framework works with autonomic mirroring and load balancing of data in database servers using MySQL master- master replication and Nginx respectively. Here nginx is used to balance the load among the database servers. It shifts the request to the appropriate DB server. Administrator keeps an eye on working of servers through Nagios tool 24X7 monitoring can't be done manually by the service provider. The proposed work has been implemented in the cloud virtualization environment. Experimental results show that our framework can deal with fault tolerance very effectively.

LIST OF FIGURES

LIST OF TABLES

TABLE OF CONTENT

CHAPTER 1

INTRODUCTION

1.1. Cloud Computing Evolution

The conception of **Cloud Computing** came into existence in 1950 with the implementation of mainframe computers, accessible via thin/static clients. Since then, cloud computing has been evolved from static clients to dynamic ones from software to services [1]. The Figure 1.1 [2] given below will explain the evolution of cloud computing:

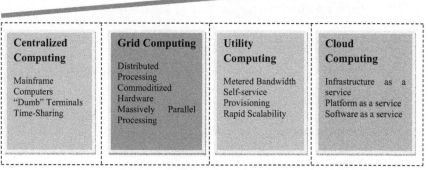

Figure 1.1: Evolution of Cloud Computing from Centralized Computing

Centralized computing came with the idea of doing the computing at the central location with the help of terminals which are connected to central computer. The computer has control over all the peripherals may be directly or may be through terminals. The centralized computing offer the large security because all of the processing is handle over the central location. Grid computing is the gathering of all computer resources from different locations to attain the specific goal [3]. Grid computing uses the approach of parallel computing to solve the large problems. Utility computing is contain the idea of metered services and has the rapid scallability because the user has to pay for the services used by it. There is no need to pay for the extra services.

1

The following Table 1.1 shows the various definitions of the cloud computing with respect to the different organizations.

Table 1.1: Definitions of Cloud computing

Author/Organization	Definition
Gartner	A way of computing through which IT related services are provided to multiple end users using internet.
Michael Brown	A data processing infrastructure in which the application software and often data reside on server's side that is connected to the internet.
Rajkumar Buyya	Cloud is a parallel and distributed system consisting of a collection of interconnected and virtualized computers that are dynamically provisioned and presented as one or more unified computing resources based on service-level agreement established through negotiation between the service provider and consumers.
National Institute of Standards and Technology (NIST)	Cloud computing is a model for enabling convenient, on demand network access to a shared pool of configurable computing resources (e.g., networks, servers, storage, applications, and services) that can be rapidly provisioned and released with minimal management effort or service provider interaction. This Cloud model is composed of five essential characteristics, three service models, and four deployment models [1].
The Open Cloud Manifesto Consortium	Style of computing by which dynamically scale and provision computing resources in cost effective way so that user can make the most without manage the underlying complexity.

1.2. Introduction to Cloud Computing

Cloud computing [4] is typically defined as the computing which includes the shared pool of resources instead of local servers. In cloud computing the word "Cloud" is the metaphor of internet so it is also known as the internet based computing [5]. It offers various services like storage, applications and platforms. There are several benefits of cloud computing like fault tolerance, reliability, on demand service and also to achieve the peak-load handling. Cloud computing provides the reliability at the greater extent by optimizing the infrastructure. Data on the cloud migrate very quickly for the availability to the user. This migration is transparent to the user. The environment for the application where these has to run should be compatible with the environment of cloud.

The following Figure 1.2 [6] shows the examples of various cloud service providers. Among all of these the Amazon is the giant cloud service provider which came into existence in 2002. It provides a number of cloud services like large computations and to storing the big data with high level security. Then after this in 2006, Amazon introduces its new product EC2 (Elastic Compute Cloud). This offers commercial we services. In 2009, the well known company Google has start offering its Cloud based services like Google Apps that offer the facilities like email, data storage and many of the shared services. The cloud providers provides various services like calendar and spread data sheet. After these Microsoft launched their own cloud Microsoft Azure in February 2010. It provides both of the service infrastructure as a service and platform as a service (PAAS) which includes business analytics, access management, data management and identity.

Figure 1.2: Top Cloud computing Services Providers

1.3. Characteristics of Cloud Computing

(i) Cost Degradation: - Cloud computing provides pay-per-use facility. It is very beneficial for the novice not to invest the large amount of money on the infrastructure and the technology. One can easily access the required data or resources for the time to use it.

(ii) Rapid Elasticity and Scalability: - Rapid elasticity provides the quick scale in and scale out of the services. This scalability helps the user to easily access the data from anywhere after paying the cost. This scalability is transparent to consumer.

(iii)Improved Reliability: - Services offered by the cloud to the users are in continuation i.e. without any interruption. High reliability is achieved by maintaining the replicas of data so that user can access it from anywhere at any time.

(iv)Measured Services: - Cloud computing provides the metered services. Users have to pay for the services they want to access. Rather than purchasing the whole software or infrastructure, one can utilise the services from cloud at anywhere and anytime. No need for the things that we don't want to use.

4

(v) Resource Pooling: - A large number of resource and service opportunities are there present in the cloud. These all services are available among all the users. Multiple users can access the same services or different at the same time from anywhere.

1.4. Cloud Computing Services

On the basis of services provided by the cloud, it has three types. It includes the knowledge about the property of the services. The different services provided by cloud are: SAAS, PAAS, IAAS has also shown in the below Figure 1.3.

1.4.1. Software as a Service (SAAS)

Saas service model is also known as a delivery model. With the help of this model multiple numbers of users can access the data or software at any time provided by the service providers. Users can access the data remotely. To run the given the software, the user can also use the Pass and Iaas services. In today's market there are various companies whom provide the software like google, Microsoft, amazon etc. Gmail is the well known example of this.

1.4.2. Platform as a Service (PAAS)

In Paas, the providers set up the platform (like API's) for the cloud users where the users can create their own applications and run (or implement) them on the infrastructure provided by the provider. There are various tools available for the users online. With the help of Paas one can create the innovative application at low cost and quickly. Google App Engine and Windows azure are famous paas offering.

5

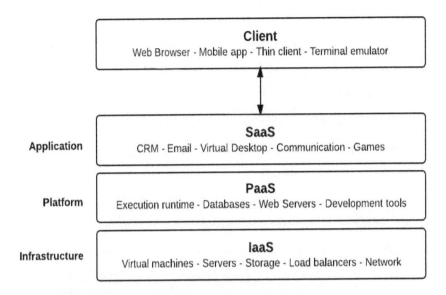

Figure 1.3: Service Models

1.4.3. Infrastructure as a Service (IAAS)

It is known as delivery service model or hardware as a service. In Iaas, the cloud providers offer various applications and resources to the users. The organizations offer the storage devices, NIC's, Processors etc. to the clients. The clients can modify their systems according to their operating system configurations and their needs. The users can create their own applications and put them on the cloud. Examples of Iaas are Amazon EC2, Nimbus, Rackspace etc.

1.5. Deployment Models of Cloud Computing

Deployment models describe the location of the cloud i.e. where the cloud is hosted. The following Figure 1.4 shows the four types of deployment models:

1.5.1. Public cloud

The public cloud is hosted by the third party or outside the vendor's premises. The services of public cloud are available and shared by the all public users. The users have no knowledge

6

about the cloud where it is hosted and who manage it. It is very cost-effective because you have to just pay for what you have to use. Examples of public cloud are Blue cloud by IBM, Google App Engine.

1.5.2. Private Cloud

Private clouds are basically for the organizations to keep the confidential data on them that they do not want to share with others. These are of two types: On-premises cloud and externally hosted cloud. In on-premises cloud, the cloud is hosted by the company itself. All of the work of data management is done by the organization. It is more secure. In the externally hosted, the cloud is hosted by the third party who works for the organization. The work of data management on cloud is done by them. Externally hosted are less expensive as compared to the on-premises. Examples are openstack, Amazon private cloud.

The Table 1.2 [7] given below describes the brief summary of deployment models.

Table 1.2: Deployment Models

Private Cloud	Public Cloud	Hybrid Cloud	Community Cloud
Used for single organization; can be externally and internally hosted	Provisioned for open use for public by a particular organization who also hosts the service	Composition of two or more clouds that remains unique entities but are bound together , offering the benefits of multiple deployment models	Shared by several organizations; typically externally hosted but may be hosted by one of the internal organization

1.5.3. Community Cloud

Community clouds are formed for the companies having the common requirements and hosted by the third party. It is also used by the organizations having the joint venture or doing work on the similar project. Example of community cloud is government organizations.

7

1.5.4. Hybrid Cloud

Hybrid cloud contains both the public cloud and the private cloud or community cloud and private cloud. Some organizations have to share some data with the other one that reside on their private cloud, then that some data is put on the public cloud for sharing which act as a hybrid cloud.

1.6. Layered Architecture of Cloud Computing

The following Figure 1.4 [8] shows the service – oriented layered design of cloud computing. The aim of user-level middleware [9] is to providing the paas capabilities. The top layer aimed to provide the software services through the services provided by the lower layer services [10]. Paas/Saas services are mostly developed and provide by the third party that are different from Iaas providers.

(i) **User-level middleware:** - The frameworks such as AJAX that helps the developers to create the attractive or cost effective user-interface applications are included in this layer. Various types of composition tools and programming environments are also include in this layer.

(ii) **Core-level middleware:** - This layer includes the programming environments that helps to run the applications built using the user-level layer. The examples of services managed at this layer are Amazon EC2, Google App Engine etc.

(iii)**System Level:** - In cloud computing the computing power required is supplied by the data centre. At this system level [11] there are large number of physical resources attached that power the data centres.

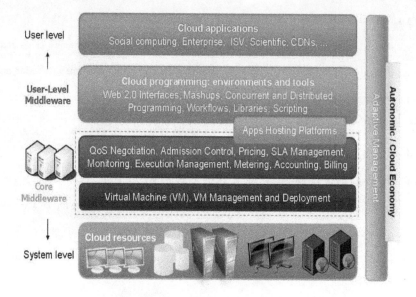

Figure 1.4: Layered Architecture

1.7. Research Issues in Cloud Computing

As cloud computing is an emerging technique in IT industry but there are some issues in it. The various research issues related to the cloud computing is following:

(i) **Data Security Issue:** As in the cloud computing due to availability of various resources the data is stored online by the clients but they do not have any knowledge about the location of data whether the data is secure or not [5], [12]. Due to this security issue data can be used by the others. Due to this many organizations feels unfriendly to share information on the cloud. It offers many technologies which require high level of security [13] like transaction management, resource scheduling etc.

(ii) **Privacy Issues:** Many organizations use the cloud infrastructure to store the data but there are privacy [14] issues in it. Sometimes due to work load the data has to migrate from one cloud to another which requires authentication. Data on public cloud is shared by the multiple users that require privacy and safety.

9

(iii)Data Management Issues: Large amount of data is stored [15] on the cloud and management of that big data is also a challenge. Most of the organizations store their data on the cloud but they don't know anything about the location of cloud where it resides. It may be in another country so it becomes difficult for the vendor to manage the data. So the chances of data stealing get increased. If the organizations want to modify the data or want to use the benefits of cloud for resource allocation then they have to consult with the third party to do the changes.

(iv)Availability Issues: It deals with the availability of the same cloud at the same time. The vendors have large clouds provided by them that are geographically spread. It is not sure that the cloud used to store the data [16] will be same next time. The vendors also don't know about the location of the data stored on the cloud, it can be anywhere in the world.

(v) Performance Issues: The performance issues in the cloud computing is to measure the performance for test and development engineers. The measuring of performance is difficult because the location of cloud is not known.

(vi)Fault Tolerance Issues: Cloud providers have to be suffering from various faults. For the system to make fault tolerable it should perform the working even after the occurrence of faults. It requires very high consideration because the infrastructure of cloud is made of various hardware and software. Moreover the data of cloud is not residing on the single data centre therefore the chances of occurrence of fault increase.

1.8. Virtualization

Virtualization is the concept of sharing the resources of one operating system with another operating system. In computing virtualization [17], [18] means to create the virtual version of resources like network interface card, processor, memory, hard disk etc. and even the operating system. It distributes the resources among two or more executable environments.

10

1.8.1. Overview of X86 Virtualization

In this X86 virtualization, a virtual layer is merged between the hardware and the operating systems for sharing the resources. The host operating system which has to share the resources among the guest operating systems install the virtual environment and runs the virtualization layer as the application on the top of the operating system, whereas the hypervisor has direct access to share the hardware resources with the operating system. The Figure 1.5 given below helps to understand the sharing of resources in X86 architecture.

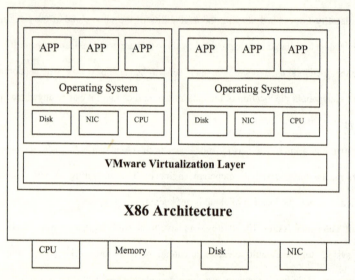

Figure 1.5: X86 Virtualization Layer

In case of **hypervisor** there is no need to run through the operating system layer. Therefore, as compared to X86 virtualization the hypervisor provides more efficient architecture. It delivers better performance, scalability and flexibility. The functionality of the hypervisor varies according to the architecture and implementation. Figure 1.6 shows the virtualization of resource using the hypervisor.

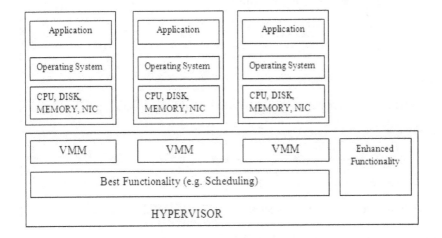

Figure 1.6: Hypervisor Manages VMM

1.8.2. CPU Virtualization

The X86 operating systems are designed in such a way that they directly run on the bare-metal hardware, so they assume that they own the full hardware of the system. In this case for the virtualization there exist the virtualization layers under the operating system to share the resources among the virtual machine.

There exist three alternative techniques for the CPU virtualization on the X86 architecture that are following:

(i)   Full Virtualization using Binary Translation

The technique binary translation and direct execution enables the vmware to do the virtualization of any X86 operating system. The instructions that cannot be virtualized are replaced with the new sequence of instructions by translating the kernel code. These new instructions have great impact on the virtual hardware. The monitor of all the virtual machines allow the virtual machines to share the services if the physical system i.e. virtual hardware and the memory management. In full virtualization, the guest operating system is not aware about

12

the virtualization and no need of any modification. There is no need of hardware support and operating system support in full virtualization to virtualize the privileged instruction.

(ii)   OS Assisted Virtualization or Paravirtualization

The word para means "beside" or "alongside". So it becomes "alongside virtualization". Paravirtualization is done to improve the efficiency during the communication between guest operating system and the hypervisor. There is some difference between full virtualization and paravirtualization because in full virtualization the guest operating is not aware of the virtual environment and for the sensitive instructions to be virtualized binary translation has been done. In paravirtualization there is no need any binary translation. The performance of the paravirtualization varies according to the workload.

(iii)   Hardware Assisted Virtualization

In hardware virtualization there is no need of any binary translation and the paravirtualization because in this the sensitive calls are set in such a way that they trap the hypervisor directly.

(a)   Memory Virtualization

After the CPU virtualization the next one is memory virtualization i.e. critical. In this the sharing of physical memory held which is dynamically allocating to the virtual machines. In today's X86 systems MMU (Memory Management Unit) is used to optimize the performance of VM's. If one has to run the multiple virtual machines on the single host operating system then memory virtualization has been done with the help of MMU.

Comparison of all the virtualization techniques described in the Table 1.3. In this the virtualization techniques of x86 processor are compared i.e. comparison between Full Virtualization, Hardware Assisted Virtualization and OS Assisted Virtualization.

13

Table 1.3: Comparison of x86 processor Virtualization Techniques

	Full Virtualization with Binary Translation	Hardware Assisted Virtualization	OS Assisted Virtualization / Paravirtualization
Technique	Binary Translation and Direct Execution	Exit to Root Mode on Privileged Instructions	Hypercalls
Guest Modification / Compatibility	Unmodified Guest OS Excellent compatibility	Unmodified Guest OS Excellent compatibility	Guest OS codified to issue Hypercalls so it can't run on Native Hardware or other Hypervisors Poor compatibility; Not available on Windows
Performance	Good	Fair Current performance lags Binary Translation virtualization on various workloads	Better in certain cases
Used By	VMware, Microsoft, Parallels	VMware, Microsoft, Parallels, Xen	VMware, Xen
Guest OS Hypervisor Independent?	Yes	Yes	XenLinux runs only on Xen Hypervisor VMI-Linux is Hypervisor agnostic

(b) Device and I/O Virtualization

The most important requirement in virtualization is the virtualization of I/O devices. The physical hardware are virtualizes by the hypervisor and provides each virtual machine a set of virtual devices. This I/O virtualization includes the sharing of the NIC's, Ethernet, sound card, USB etc.

1.9. Introduction to Fault Tolerance

A system is said to be fault tolerable if the system keeps on working even after the occurrence of fault like failure of any component, it may be hardware or software. Even if it not able to remove the fault [19], [20] but it still permit the system to perform the task at low efficiency and reduced rate.

1.9.1. Importance of Fault Tolerance in Cloud Environment

Cloud computing is an emerging technique in today's scenario so it also become possible to run the real time applications on the cloud environment [21], [22]. The advantage of cloud computing i.e. scalability makes the real time applications to take the benefit of cloud computing. For the real time applications [23] to run over the cloud it is very necessary to make it fault tolerable and efficient otherwise the chances of data lose increases at a greater rate. As in the real time computing the work is done with the time bonding. So the system should have to perform the task within given time without any latency or data lose. For the system to make fault tolerable the technique used is 'replication'.

1.9.2. Management of Fault tolerance

In the working system fault can be occur at anytime at any stage. In the cloud computing environment there are three types of fault tolerance management techniques used.

(i) **Application Fault Tolerance:** This type of the fault is occurring at the consumer level. The technique applied for the recovering of the fault depends upon the nature of the application. For the applications to be working in the failure stage, sensors are attached

15

with all applications that are special software deploy by the consumer. The sensor executes the method for the repairing of application to recover the fault.

(ii) Virtual Machine Fault Tolerance: The virtual machine FT occurs at both sides: at consumer level and cloud provider level. At the consumer side the fault is repaired by the sensors which check the virtual machine [24] during the lifetime but the problem is that if the VM fails then chances of failure of sensor also gets increased. Then the fault can be repaired in the following manner:

(a) It request for new VM.

(b) Send the request to cloud to free the failed VM.

At the cloud provider level the VM [25] faults are repaired more accurately than at the consumer level. At the cloud provider level all the VM's share the single hypervisor. In contrast to VM FT at consumer level it has decreased number of VM sensors because all the sensors are integrated in the same hypervisor [24]. It decreases the time complexity.

(iii)Physical Machine Fault Tolerance: The detection of hardware failure at the consumer level is difficult to recover because this type of failure is visible is only at the consumer side. The sensors deployed in the VM's cannot repair the fault. All of the virtual machines get failed with the failure of the physical machine. For the systems to make fault recoverable the consumers should deploy the some restrictions on the location of the sensors, which integrates between the both cloud provider and consumer. At the cloud provider the hardware failure can be repaired by shifting the entire work load on the new system. In this the check points are applied at the VM's that the new system start working from the point where the failure occurs.

1.9.3. Fault Tolerance Techniques

For the systems to make fault tolerable, there exist various fault tolerance techniques. A system is said to be fault tolerable if it keeps on performing the task even after the occurrence of fault. These fault tolerance techniques are applied during the development of the cloud. First is the reactive technique, in which the faults are removed after its occurrence. The various techniques lies under this technique are Replication, job migration, retry, Check point/Restart, SGuard etc. In checkpoint/Restart, it restarts the work from the point where it gets failed. The fault has not got removed completely; there is the probability of occurrence of fault. On the other hand, the pro-active techniques of fault tolerance [26] are used to remove the fault before the job to start. It predicts the fault before occurring it and repairs it. The main advantage of pro-active fault tolerance is that it is used to remove the faults on the distinct applications [27]. The policy of pro-active fault tolerance is to predict the faults before occurring them repair them and replace or change the suspicious component with the new one. This FT can be achieved with software rejuvenation, self-healing and pre-emptive migration. The explanation of all the above techniques is as follows:

(i) **Checkpoint/Restart:** The checkpoint is used when the task completely fails then it restarts the task from the point where it gets failed. Check points are applied in it which helps it start from the failing node rather from the beginning [28].

(ii) **Replication:** Various replicas of the task are maintained which run on the different resources which can be used when one of the task get failed then other can be used.

(iii) **SGuard:** To recover the fault it used the rollback technique. With this more resources can be available.

(iv) **Job migration:** In this job is migrated on another machine or server when it gets failed [29].

17

(v) Retry: It is the technique that used to run again the failed task on the same cloud resources or machine.

(vi) Pro-active FT using Self-Healing: In the self-healing technique multiple instances are run on the multiple machines and use any of the instances to recover the fault [30], [31].

(vii)   Self-Rejuvenation: Self-rejuvenation deals with restart the system with clean state. In this system reboots itself to recover the fault [32].

(viii)   Pre-emptive Migration: It works is continuous loop manner that it checks or analyze the application in a loop [33].

1.10. Structure of Thesis

The various chapters in the thesis are arranged in the following manner

Chapter 2: This chapter of the thesis explains the existing research and literature survey in detail.

Chapter 3: This chapter describes the problem statement, objectives, framework design, interaction diagram and the implementation of the framework.

Chapter 4: This chapter includes the result of the given approach.

Chapter 5: This chapter includes the future scope and conclusion of the given approach.

CHAPTER 2
LITERATURE SURVEY

Hines et al. (2009) in the paper presented the technique for the post-copy migration of virtual machines across the gigabit LAN. In this it postpone the migration of virtual machines contents until the processor state sent to the target host. In this post-copy migration is compared with the pre-copy migration. Post-copy migration provides the win-win strategy which reduces the time during migration by maintaining the liveliness of the virtual migrations. In contrast to pre-copy, it first copies the content using the multiple iterations and the sent to the final host.

Sidiroglou et al. (2009) represented the technique which includes the rescue points that help in recover the fault in softwares. The fault can be of any type i.e. unknown faults. These faults occur while maintaining the availability and the system integrity. For recovery it mimics the system behaviour under the known conditions of errors. As it uses the rescue points to restore the execution at a particular point and helps the program to run after recovery.

Kaushal and Bala (2010) presented in their paper a fault tolerance solution to handle the faults at the customer level by maintaining the replication the server queries. In this they used the haproxy as a load balancer. The given work is only applicable for the saas cloud here is not any partition between the cloud provider and the customer.

Zhao et al. (2010) represented the idea of Low Latency Fault Tolerance (LLFT). The LLFT provides the fault tolerance for the distributed applications using the leader/follower approach. It consists of low latency messaging protocol, a virtual determinizer framework and a leader – determined membership protocol. The messaging protocol provides the reliable, ordered message directly group to group multicast. The virtual determinizer captures the ordering at the primary replica and enforces the backup to maintain the replicas. The recovery and the reconfiguration service are provided by the membership protocol when any replica is faulty. The LLFT maintains the replication consistency and end-to-end latency.

19

Hamlen et al. (2010) proposed the idea in paper is related to the security issues in cloud computing. A layered framework has been proposed to secure the cloud in which two layers are mianly explained that kare storage layer and data layer. Next the paper has discussed the secure query processing using the hadoop and the map reduce technique. Finally the author has explained the XACML implementation for hadoop. With this one can use the untrusted componenets with the trusted applications for the secure cloud computing.

Tan et al. (2010) proposed the model which provides the replication approach for virtual machine fault tolerance. As mainly virtual machine failures are managed by the cloud providers. This model using the passive VM replicas that helps in improving the efficiency by using vary few resources. These passive replicas gets activate when any of the failure occurs. The mechanism for transfer/initialize the VM is also introduced.

Kumar (2011) discussed in their paper the idea of message exchanging among processors. The aim is to development of communication network that uses the TDMA-style which avoids the message from the interference of the faulty processors and ensures the non-faulty processors to get the message. A component is used here to prevent the faulty processor to speak outside the given slot. In TTP/C this component is known as guardian.

Malik and Huet (2011) described the execution of real time applications using the cloud infrastructure. Most of the cloud applications are remote based in which the chances of errors are more. They proposed the model for real time tasks which perform the implementation by checking the reliability of the virtual machines. The reliability of virtual machine is adaptive if it produces the correct result after each computation. If the virtual machine able to give the correct result within the given time limits then its reliability increases. There is more chance of decrease in the reliability rather than increase. If the node keeps on decreasing then there is need to change the node. The main motive of this technique is to check the adaptive reliability of the nodes by adding the weights.

Tchana et al. (2012) discussed that the FT in cloud computing is the very crucial issue. Since cloud computing is splitting into many different layers. They discussed that the in most of the FT approaches the work is done at the customer level or at the server side that does not work efficiently but on their experimental result they have used the collaborative approach for the autonomic cloud computing fault tolerance.

Bala (2012) proposed in their paper that fault tolerance is the major concern in the implementation and reliability of the application. They proposed that the fault should be pro-actively tolerated or handled. They discuss the various existing fault tolerance tools, their policies and research challenges. In the proposed experimental result they used the virtualized system and shows that how to overcome the software fault.

Singh and Singh (2012) proposed the two tier scheme for the authentication of data over the cloud. In the cloud computing there are many security issues related to it for finanacial transactions, personal information etc. To recover the drawback of security issue in cloud they have used two tiers. The one tier contains the username and the password or the next tier consist of some predetermined number of steps. With this one achieve the security in cloud upto some extent and moreover there is no need to use the additional hardwares.

Das and Dr. Khilar (2013) represented that the detection and recovery are the main fault tolerance issues in cloud computing. In the proposed technique they have used the virtualization and fault tolerance technique. A cloud manager and the decision maker are used in this to handle the faults and to manage the virtualization and the load balancing. VFT is mainly designed to handle the reactive FT. In this the fault handler is used which blocks the unrecoverable faulty nodes along with their virtual nodes for future requests.

Gupta and Bala (2013) proposed the fault tolerence technique to reassure the system availability and the system reliability. In this technique system keeps on woring even after the

21

detection of fault. Haproxy tool has been used in this paper for the fault tolerence. This tool automatically detect the fault and shift the load on the another server for the system reliability. Jhawar et al. (2013) in their paper in the given paper they have described the modular, innovative, system level perspective on creating and managing the FT in cloud. They have implemented the high level result for the fault tolerance at the service layer and for the application developers, users at the service layer. The service layer allows the user to apply the fault tolerance at the desired level but does not give any details about the fault tolerance implementations.

Lakshmi (2013) discussed the fault tolerance techniques for the real time applications. In real time application it is critical to manage the reliability. In the proposed model they have manage the fault on the basis of the reliability of the virtual machines which based on the design diverse variants on the multiple virtual machines and assigning the reliability on the basis of resulting variants. The system provides both the backward and the forward recovery mechanism.

Ganesh et al. (2014) proposed the various fault tolerance techniques to make the system fault tolerable. To provide the continuous availability of data and resources, it is a big challenge to make the system fault tolerable. In this paper various fault tolerance techniques has been highlighted like reactive FT and Proactive FT. Various frameworks, algorithms are discussed which are used by the experts in this field.

Summary

In the literature review various authors has described various different methods for the security related to the cloud and for the fault tolerance in cloud computing. Some of the authors discussed the different fault tolerance techniques and tools. The fault tolerance techniques discussed are the reactive fault tolerance and the proactive FT. The tools mainly used for the fault tolerance are hadoop and haproxy. Some authors have represents the authentication scheme and the migration of virtual machines for the fault tolerance. After studying all these papers some gaps are analysed. For the efficient reliability and the availability of data there is need to maintain the replica of data at the server ends. With the load balancing of web servers for the availability of applications, it can be done at the backend servers to balance the load among them. Work load can be reduced by applying the approach of automatic monitoring of database servers which is a very difficult job to do it manually.

CHAPTER 3

PRESENT WORK

3.1. Problem Definition

Existing literature covers distributed architectures to cover fault tolerance which inherently covers data transmission delay and communication response. Detecting fault and replicating entire system image is typically a hard job to achieve. However, the replication can be performed but with much delay. On the other side client has to wait tremendous amount of time so recovery still possible but with large response time. Our research focus on similar kind of replication techniques based upon mirror cloning in single standalone system where proactive measures has been deployed to check system performance degradation. The level of degradation just before unresponsive behaviour of system state is detected and the present workload is spread out to the scaled system deployed. Although number of concurrent request are scheduled according to the efficiency of the current intended systems. The Figure 3.1 shows the traditional approach used for the data transmission.

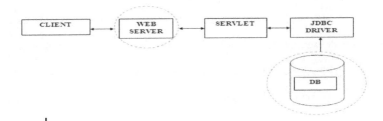

Figure 3.1: Traditional Approach

The Problem is to tolerate the fault if any of the servers goes down.

(i) For this, there is need to insert the large number of web servers and DB servers.

(ii) To shift the load on secondary servers if the primary one fails.

24

(iii)To maintain the replication mirroring of the data at the server end to provide the efficient data.

(iv)To use the monitoring tool that will alert the user about the commencement of failure by sending the mail and sms 24X7.

3.2.   Objectives

The objective of the given proposed problem is to handle or manage the fault before occurring it and maintain the replication of the data. In the given problem we have to use the proactive fault tolerance to recover the fault. There is also use the monitoring tool to send the notification to the user.

The main objectives are:

(i) To design the framework which detect the fault i.e. to find the overloaded server and shift the load on the secondary server.

(ii) To design the system which automatic maintain the replica at server end.

(iii)To monitor the DB servers repository with in depth data hierarchy.

3.3.   Framework Design

The proposed model of FT is shown below in the figure. This framework provides FT and better QoS to the web applications which will run on the cloud environment. Since the use of data replication, load balancing and monitoring, OS-level virtualization has been done for the applications to be run in the fault tolerable environment. For the data to be available for the users if strike at the same time OS-level virtualization has been done which creates the dynamic image of the whole system and implement in the same manner application works. For the data to be secure in the database and to be available for the user 24X7, master-master replication has been done. The FT can be ensured up to greater extent for the system to be reliable. The framework design has been explain in the Figure 3.2 shown below.

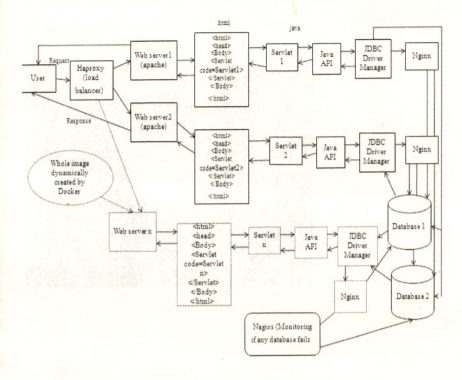

Figure 3.2: Framework Design

3.3.1 Vmware Workstation

Vmware Workstation is a tool used for the virtualization. This tool mainly used to share resources of host operating system with the guest operating system. User can install the number of guest operating systems according to the requirements and also use the resources with respect to the need. One can customize the settings like which memory Space, disk sharing etc. In this thesis vmware workstation 11 has been used and the following Figure 3.3 and Figure 3.4 shows the images of virtualization and the customization settings of virtual machines.

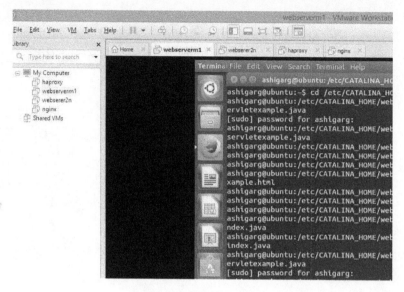

Figure 3.3: Virtualization

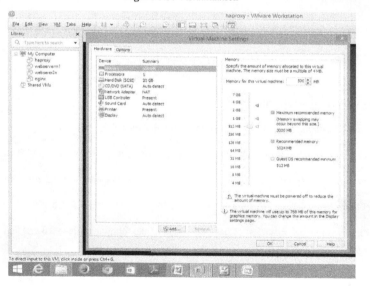

Figure 3.4: Virtual Machine Settings

3.3.2 Ubuntu

Ubuntu is an operating system based on the Linux and the Debian GNU. It is free and open source software. Anyone can get it online. Ubuntu is used for the desktop of PCs. In the given thesis ubuntu 14.04 is used. Here four ubuntu has been installed on the vmware.

3.3.3 Haproxy

Haproxy meant for High Availability Proxy and used for balancing the load among various web servers or database servers [34]. The services that are located in the cloud environment can be accessed by the user using the application layer. This user interface is created by using HTML that helps us to control the data to be sent as input. The user will first interact with the HAProxy and then HAProxy [10] will forward the request using the upstream module, In order to send the data through web browser, where our web page has been loaded. The data is being passed to the web server and then finally to the program which is running at the background. It is this layers from which load balancer receives the request and forwards it to a particular web server. After receiving the request from the application layer the load balancer i.e. haproxy forwards the request to a particular web server as per the *weight* option. This weight option acts as priority indicator. According to the configurations of machine i.e. their computation powers which are running web servers the weight can be assigned accordingly.

- **HAProxy Configuration**

  The configuration file of haproxy mainly consists of three major parameters:

  (i) Command line arguments, precedence always assign to it.

  (ii) Global section describes the parameters which have to be used process-wide.

  (iii)The section after the global section is assign to proxies which includes the 'default', 'frontend', 'backend' and 'listen'.

  #haproxy.cfg

  global

28

```
log 127.0.0.1              local0

log 127.0.0.1              local1 notice

maxconn                    5000

chroot                     /var/lib/haproxy

user                       haproxy

group                      haproxy

daemon

defaults

log                        global

mode                       http

option                     httplog

option                     dontlognull

option                     redispatch

retries                    3

maxconn                    4000

contimeout                 5000

clitimeout                 50000

srvtimeout                 50000

listen                     LOADBAL 192.168.206.154:1991

mode                       http

cookie                     LOADBAL insert

balance                    roundrobin

option                     httpclose

option                     forwardfor

server                     webserver1 192.168.206.152:80 check weight 2
```

server	webserver2 192.168.206.149:80 check
listen	stats *:1991
mode	http
stats	enable
stats	hide-version
stats	realm Haproxy\ Statistics
stats	uri /
stats	auth ashigarg:ashima

The web interface page of haproxy is shown in Figure 3.5. It is authentication page in which admin has to enter the user name and password to access the statistic report.

Figure 3.5: Authentication Page for Haproxy

3.3.4 Docker

The open-source project Docker [35] helps in the deployment of the application within the software container by offering the further layer of abstraction and automation of operating system using OS-level-virtualization. Docker can easily run on number of platforms so one can easily deploy the applications anywhere like on virtual machines, physical servers, public cloud etc.

3.3.5   Servlet Application

A java program developed using javax.servlet and javax.servlet.http package known as Servlet which deploys on web servers and acts as a core between web browsers request or HTTP clients and HTTP servers or different databases. Using servlet user can easily communicate with other softwares by making use of RMI, socket. After the request has been processed it is forwarded to the database. Java API and JDBC driver manager helps in making connection with the database by providing specific drivers as per the database requirements.

3.3.6   Nginx

Nginx [36] well known for its better performance, stability, simple   configuration, and low memory usage etc. It is a load balancer for servers. The JDBC driver forwards the request to the Nginx for the appropriate database server to store the data. After this the Nginx check the status of both the MySQL database server used and shift the load among them in the roundrobin fashion and also shift the load priority wise which is assigned by the weight option. The Figure 3.6 given below shows the configuration details of the nginx.

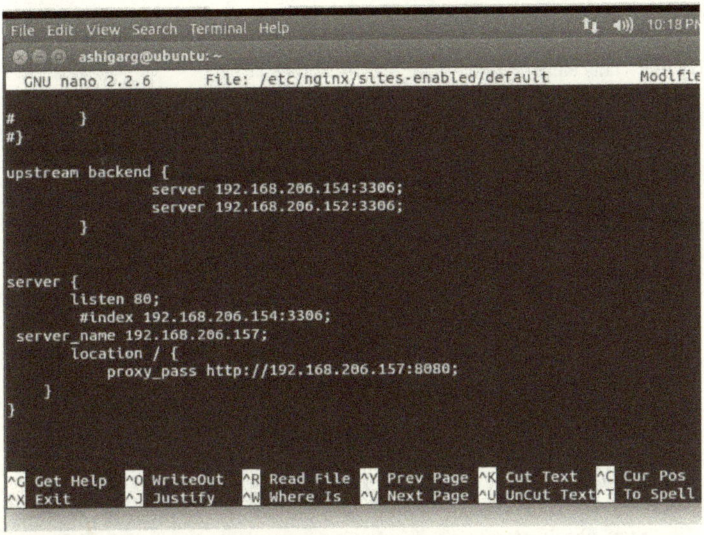

Figure 3.6: Configuration File of Nginx

3.3.7 MySQL Database

In order to add redundancy and speed for the active websites the MySQL master-master replication is performed [37]. The replication of MySQL results in cluster formation which helps in attaining the high availability website configuration. For doing the master-master replication changes has to be done in the configuration file of the MySQL i.e. *my.cnf*. The final replication is done by copying the *master status* of both the servers, which gets all the information about the DB which has to be copied. The data that has to be copied across servers for performing replications are *server's IP address, user, password, log file* etc.

3.3.8 Nagios

Nagios [10] is an open source monitoring tool which helps in monitoring network services like SMTP, POP3, and NNTP etc. checking the parallelized services, contact notifications whenever some problem gets resolved or problem arises. A plugin *check_mysql_health* helps in monitoring the MySQL database. It displays the statistic report of the servers which has to be monitored. In the report, it shows the status of servers, host and services. The various metrics

32

which can be monitored are connection-time, uptime, threads-connected, slow-queries, slave-sql-running, log-waits etc.

Nagios has been designed in the way to provide the web interface and has various plugins installed in it used to monitor the various services. The changes have been made in the configuration file of the nagios.

define host {

use	**generic-host**
host_name	**mysql1**
alias	**mysqlserver1**
address	**192.168.206.154**
max_check_attempts	**5**
check_period	**24x7**
notification_interval	**30**
notification_period	**24x7**

}

define host {

use	**generic-host**
host_name	**mysql2**
alias	**mysqlserver2**
address	**192.168.206.152**
max_check_attempts	**5**
check_period	**24x7**
notification_interval	**30**
notification_period	**24x7**

}

3.4. Interaction Diagram

The interaction diagram is used to show the interaction among the different elements and flow of messages. Stepwise implementation has also been discussed in this section. The solution for the given problem that is how to make the system fault tolerable is described in this section. The interaction diagram shows in Figure 3.7 explains the workflow of the current approach.

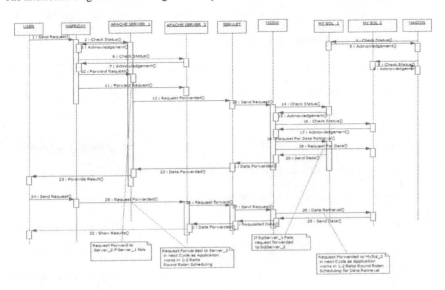

Figure 3.7: Interaction Diagram

3.5. Implementation of the Framework

The complete framework for the given present work is designed with the use of VMware workstation. VMware workstation 11.0 has been used for the purpose of virtualization. After installing the vmware on the windows host operating system, four ubuntu 14.04 guest operating systems installed on it. In the present work we have used two apache tomcat servers on two different ubuntu for the web application to run online. The programming language of the web application is java servlet program. On the third ubuntu, haproxy has been installed, which act as a load balancer. Haproxy balance the load among these two apache web servers. For the data

34

to be stored, mysql servers have been used. We have use two mysql servers on different guest operating systems. The purpose of using the two database servers is to provide the efficient data to the user all time. The data provided by it is consistent and flexible because it done the master-master replication at backend. The data stored on the one DB server will be copied to another DB server. For balancing the load among the database servers, nginx has been used. Nginx can be used as web server, load balancer, etc. in the present work nginx used to check the availability of the database servers. It forwards the request to the appropriate server. The monitoring tool nagios is used for admin to check the status of database servers. The nagios tool gives the acknowledgment to the admin 24x7. It checks the database servers in the deep hierarchy.

(i) **Client_request:** At the very first client will send the request by entering the domain name or the IP address specified for the application to run. The request will be forwarded through the HAProxy server to the web servers without getting into the knowledge of client. Haproxy used here performing the job of balancing the load among the servers. If any of the server goes down or having the overload then haproxy shift the load among another servers used in contrast with that server. It performs the task or balances the load in proactive manner i.e. it detects or configures the load before occurring it. It configures the fault itself ones the admin have to just do the modifications in the configuration file.

(ii) **Balancing incoming requests among the web servers:** After getting request from the user the task of the HAProxy is to check the availability of the web servers and to balance the load among the web servers that are hooked up with HAProxy. The HAProxy will forward the request to the appropriate server according to their priority .These priorities are assigned in the configuration file with the help of weight option, so as to distribute the load as per the systems configuration available such as 1:2 fashion.

35

The HAProxy will also check whether the servers are working properly or not. If any of the server will goes down then in the statistics report generated by HAProxy same can be highlighted using the red color. Green color corresponding to the particular server shows smooth working of the server. The following is the configuration file of haproxy which shows the details of web servers that are attached through IP addresses and the priority assigned to them. The IP mention above in the file is the IP of haproxy which helps the user to run the web application.

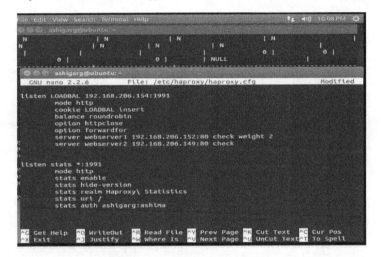

Figure 3.8: Configuration file of HAProxy

(iii) Operating system level virtualization: Although the load has been efficiently balanced by the HAProxy, in a particular case in which the number of user requests are so much that given number of available servers are not capable of handling the requests then in such case use of Docker can be done. Docker performs the virtualization at the operating system level. Docker helps us in such a way so that we can separate our application from our given infrastructure and can treat our infrastructure in a managed way. Using Docker we become capable such that image known as Docker image can be generated so that it can hold our application. Then with the help of Docker containers we can run our application by making the use of Docker image initially created. As a result dynamically more number of web servers can be deployed using the Docker images, so that the entire incoming load can be managed properly.

(iv) **Servlet Working**: Servlet is basically a java program. After getting the request for a particular servlet through a web server, the corresponding servlet is called. In a Servlet the coding for making the connection with the database i.e. JDBC through Nginx is performed. Use of Java API and Driver manager is done so that database's driver's requirement as per the particular database can be fulfilled. All the database interaction requests are forwarded to the Nginx, which is acting as a load balancer for handling the requests. The main aim of servlet is to call the JDBC driver which further calls the appropriate database server.

(v) **Load Balancing using Nginx while interacting with the database**: Nginx can be used as a web server, proxy server and the load balancer. In our work nginx has been used as a load balancer. After getting the request from the particular servlet the JDBC forwards the request to the nginx. By using Nginx as a load balancer we got a mechanism such that we can distribute the incoming traffic load i.e. the database requests among the different DB as per our requirements such as 1:2, 1:3 etc. all of the connectivity of databases with the nginx has been done in the configuration file and priority assign to them with weight option. In this the name of server which has to be used to balance the load is specified with its IP address, name of the database which has to replicate or shift among the servers, user of DB server, Password assigned, etc. By default it balances the load among the servers in round-robin fashion. One can change the algorithm with its requirements. This distribution of load can be decided as per the configurations of the virtual machines available on which database is loaded. Thus distributing the requests among various machines provides FT by ensuring stability, redundancy to the application.

#nginx configuration

http {

....

#simple round-robin

Server 192.168.206.154:3306 bname=test1 password=ashima user=root protocol=mysql;

Server 192.168.206.152:3306 dbname=test1 password=ashima user=root protocol=mysql;

}

(vi) Performing replication of Database: FT corresponding to the database is performed by performing MySQL Master-Master Replication. Nginx performs the operation of balancing the of database requests among these servers. The proposed frame work is best suited when number of incoming database queries are mainly consist of read operations. Although it can also handle queries related to write operation in database. If our application is such that the number of write operations are not very much frequent and application has to deal with mainly view operations for the user then using this proposed work we can increase our users up to much greater extent. For doing the master-master replication on the database servers changes has been done in the configuration file of both servers. It starts replicating the data after copying the master status of both servers in one another. The name of database which has to be copied is mentioned in the file my.cnf. The lines in the configuration file are shown below which has to be modified.

#my.cnf

Server-id   =   1

Log_bin   =   /var/log/mysql/mysql-bin.log

Binlog_do_db =   test1

bind-address =   127.0.0.1

The Figure 3.9 shows the master status of the database which has to be copied.

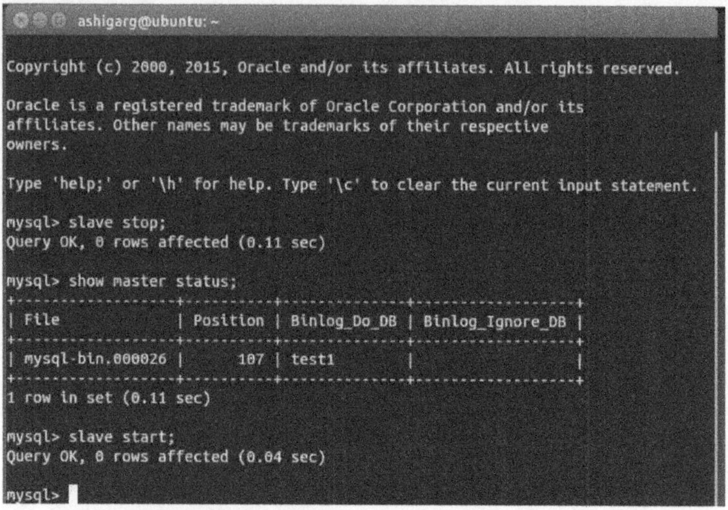

Figure 3.9: Showing the master status

After copying the master status of both the databases in one another, the replication of data starts. Data must be entered in the same database which has been mentioned in the configuration file, whether it is coming from any geographical region.

(vii)   Monitoring of MySql: Since a database has large number of entries stored in it. Manually it is very difficult to check any discrepancy in the database. Nagios has been used as a monitoring tool for the purpose of FT. Nagios will acknowledge the administrator about the status of the database server whether it is working properly or not. It sends the notification to the user through SMS, email etc. So administrator will somehow able to perform 24X7 monitoring.

CHAPTER 4

RESULTS AND DISCUSSION

This section will discuss about the experimental results of the prototype made for the FT. For the purpose of FT the given approach provides many provisions to the application so that dynamic changes can be done during deployment. These provisions are as follows:-

(i) For the purpose of easy and quick spin of a newly created web server instance and clasp into our load balancer, the use of HAProxy plus Docker has done. Docker provides operating system level virtualization; new instance of the whole application can be created dynamically by the Docker containers.

(ii) The load can be managed using the priority settings for a particular web server by High Availability proxy using the *weight* option. The incoming requests from the users can be redirected to another server if one of the servers fails to handle the request

(iii)Use of Nginx as a load balancer at the backend helps in balancing the database requests so that database operations can be divided among the replicated servers   in a better fashion.

(iv)The multiple MySQL has been made to work as a single cluster using the replication techniques. As a result a replicated copy will always be there for providing FT.

(v) Since we are having cluster of two databases. The faults like data integrity, data lost, data consistency related to database management can be minimized a lot.

(vi)The prediction of the fault and the continuous monitoring has been done using Nagios. It acknowledges the administrator 24X7 about the status of large database servers because on can't handle it manually.

The following Figure 4.1 shows the statistic report of haproxy for the balancing of the web servers. The servers which are working properly are indicating with the green line, if any of the servers goes down then red line appear on that server's name.

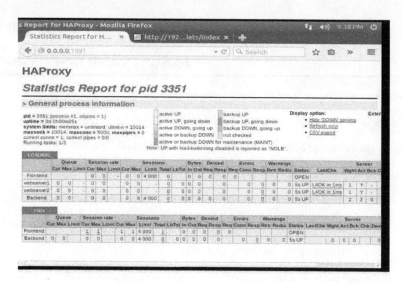

Figure 4.1: Statistic Report of Haproxy

The following Figure 4.2 represents the case in which one server goes down and it is indicating with the help of red line.

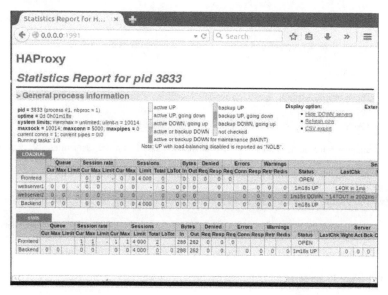

Figure 4.2 : Statistic Report of Haproxy with one server down

41

The application which has to run on the web server interacts with web server through haproxy as shown in Figure 4.3. For this the user enters the IP address of the haproxy which is declared in the configuration file of the haproxy. After opening the web page through the haproxy the servlet page send the request to the JDBC driver. JDBC driver is used to do the connectivity with the database servers. In the present work Nginx is used to balance the load among the database servers, so the request will first go to the nginx and then nginx shift the load on the available server.

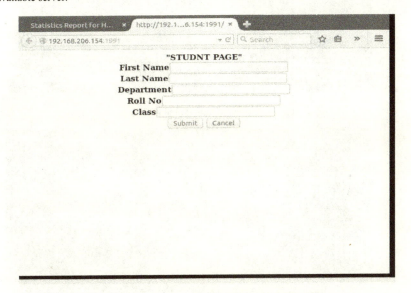

Figure 4.3: Application Running through HAProxy

After getting the request from the nginx server the data stores in the suitable mysql database server.

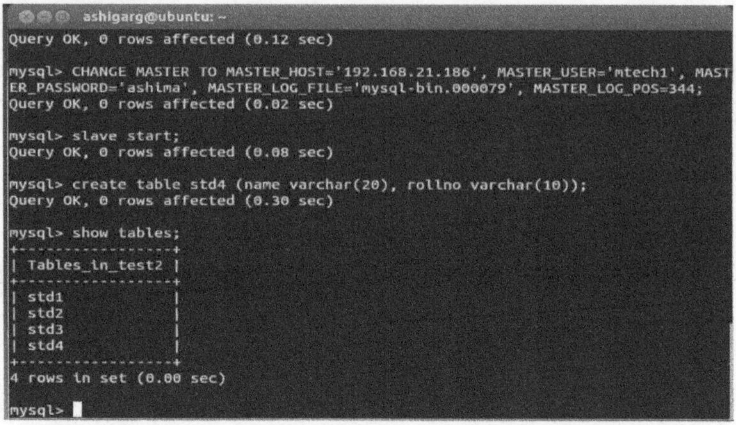

Figure 4.4: Data entered in one database

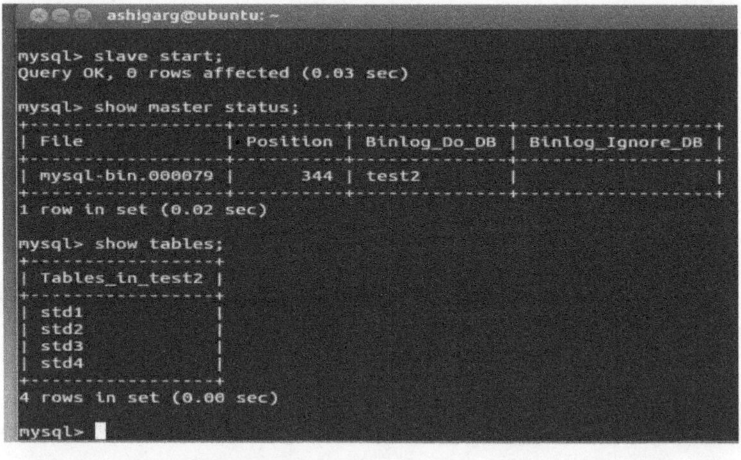

Figure 4.5: Data copied on another server

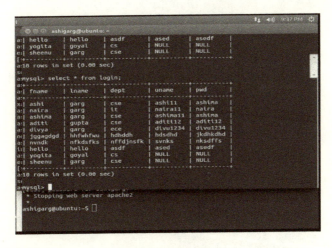

Figure 4.6: Database Entries

The monitoring of database servers is done with the help of nagios tool. The nagios tool 24x7 do the monitoring of servers and sends the acknowledgement to the admin. It tells about the status of the database servers. It shows the result in the form of statistic report. In this the green line indicates that the all the database servers are working properly, if one of the server goes down then nagios indicate it with critical state and red line. It checks the data in databases in deep hierarchy.

Figure 4.7: Statistic Report of Nagios

44

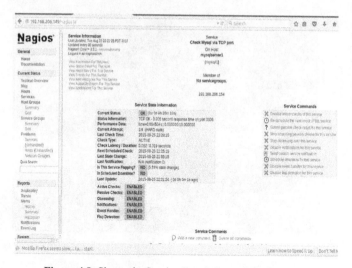

Figure 4.8: Shows the Service State Information of server 1

To start and stop the nginx one can run the commands on terminal as shown in Figure 4.9.

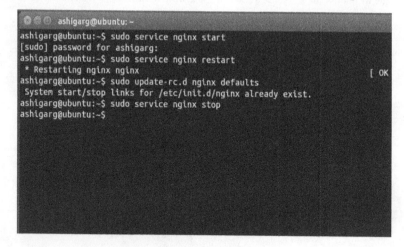

Figure 4.9: Commands on Terminal

45

CHAPTER 5
CONCLUSIONS AND FUTURE SCOPE

In this thesis the proposed framework and implementation provides the fault tolerance by ensuring reliability, scalability and availability. The result shows when unexpected traffic spikes, organic traffic growth or internal challenge like server failure or urgent maintenance of component occurs, they can be handled easily using HAProxy. It balances the load between servers. It also redirects the load to another web server when one of the web servers faces unexpected failure. Docker provides the operating system level virtualization by separation of application from the system. Master-master replication technique successfully maintains the mirror copy of database servers. Nginx balance the load in 1:2 between database servers and also redirect the respective request when one of the servers fails. Nagios enables the automatic monitoring of servers which increase accuracy and efficiency. For the future the HAProxy can be used to handle the request for multiple applications coming from the multiple users at the same time. In future one can make the system more reliable by offering the multiple applications. For example using the same haproxy server to handle the more than one services or applications running on large number of servers. To increase the efficiency of database servers, DB locks can be used. More effective use of os-level virtualization has to be done.

REFERENCES

[1] P. Mell and T. Grance, "The NIST Definition of Cloud Computing," NIST, 2011.

[2] "Evolution of cloud," [Online]. Available: http://www.slideshare.net/sagaroceanic11/. [Accessed 2015].

[3] J. Balasangameshwara and N. Raju, "A hybrid policy for fault tolerant load balancing in grid computing environments," *Journal of Network and Computer Applications*, vol. 35, no. 1, pp. 412-422, 2011.

[4] J. Sabogal, "Cloud Computing and Life Science IT," L&T Infotech, 2013.

[5] "Cloud computing issues and impacts," ey.com, [Online]. Available: http://assets-production.govstore.service.gov.uk/. [Accessed 2015].

[6] "Top cloud service providers," [Online]. Available: http://javarevisited.blogspot.in (javarevisited). [Accessed 2015].

[7] "Deployment models," [Online]. Available: http://blog.sysfore.com/ (sysfore Blog). [Accessed 2015].

[8] "Layered Architecture of cloud computing," [Online]. Available: http://dextraconsultinggroup.com/. [Accessed 2015].

[9] W. Zhao, P. M. Melliar-Smith and L. E. Moser, "Fault Tolerance Middleware for Cloud Computing," in *International Conference on Cloud Computing (CLOUD)*, 2010.

[10] D. Gupta and A. Bala, "Autonomic Fault Tolerant Framework for Web Applications," *International Journal of Computer Science and Telecommunication (IJCST)*, vol. 4, no. 2, pp. 528-533, 2013.

[11] R. Jhawar, V. Puiri and M. Santambrogio, "A Comprehensive Conceptual System-Level Approach to Fault Tolerance in Cloud Computing," in *Systems Conference (SysCon)*, 2012.

[12] K. Hamlen, M. Kantarcioglu, L. Khan and B. Thuraisingham, "Security Issues for cloud computing," *International Journal of Information Security and Privacy*, vol. 4, no. 2, pp. 39-51, 2010.

[13] S. Kumar and A. Ganpati, "Multi-authentication for cloud security: A framework," *International Journal of Computer Science & Engineering Technology*, vol. 5, no. 4, pp. 295-303, 2014.

[14] M. Singh and S. Singh, "Design and implementation of multi-tier authentication scheme in cloud," *International Journal of Computer Science Issues, IJCSI*, vol. 9, no. 5, pp. 181-187, 2012.

[15] Q. Feng, J. Han, Y. Gao and D. Meng, "Magicube: High Reliability and Low Redundancy Storage Architecture for Cloud Computing," in *International Conference on Networking, Architecture, and Storage*, 2012.

[16] J. Kaur and S. Bagga, "Hybrid Model of RSA, AES and Blowfish to enhance Cloud Security," *International Journal of Computers and Technology*, vol. 14, no. 9, pp. 6059-6066, 2015.

[17] P. Das and P. M. Khilar, "VFT: A Virtualization and Fault Tolerance Approach for Cloud Computing," in *In Information and Communication Technologies (ICT)*, 2013.

[18] U. Tan, D. Luo and J. Wang, ""Cc-vit: Virtualization intrusion tolerance based on cloud computing," in *International Conference on Information Engineering and Computer Science (ICIECS)*, Wuhan, China, 2010.

[19] A. Ganesh, M. Sandhya and S. Shankar, "A Study on Fault Tolerance methods in Cloud Computing," in *In Advance Computing Conference (IACC)*, 2014.

[20] S. S. Lakshmi, "Fault Tolerance in Cloud Computing," *International Journal of Engineering Sciences Research*, vol. 4, no. 1, pp. 1285-1288, 2013.

[21] A. Tchana, L. Broto and D. Hagimont, "Approaches to Cloud Computing Fault Tolerance," in *Computer, Information and Telecommunication Systems (CITS)*, 2012.

[22] A. Bala and I. Chana, "Fault Tolerance- Challenges, Techniques and Implementation in Cloud Computing," *International Journal of Computer Science Issues (IJCSI)*, vol. 9, no. 1, pp. 288-293, 2012.

[23] S. Malik and F. Huet, "Adaptive Fault Tolerance in Real Time Computing," in *IEEE World Congress on Services (SERVICES)*, 2011.

[24] F. Ma, F. Liu and Z. Liu, "Live Virtual Machine Migration Based on Improved Precopy Approach," in *Software Engineering and Service Sciences*, 2010.

[25] M. R. Hines, U. Deshpande and K. Gopalan, "Post-Copy Live Migration of Virtual Machine," *ACM SIGOPS Operating Systems Review*, vol. 43, no. 3, pp. 14-26, 2009.

[26] P. Kumar, "Abstract Model of Fault Tolerance Algorithm in Cloud Computing Communication Networks," *International Journal on Computer Science and Engineering*, vol. 3, no. 9, pp. 3283-3290, 2011.

[27] G. Chen, H. Jin, D. Zou, B. B. Zhou, W. Qiang and G. Hu, "SHelp: Automatic Self-healing for Multiple Application Instances in a Virtual Machine Environment," in *IEEE International Conference on Cluster Computing*, 2010.

[28] G. Belalem and S. Limam, "Fault Tolerant Architecture to Cloud Computing Using Adaptive Checkpoint," *International Journal of Cloud Applications and Computing*, vol. 1, no. 4, pp. 60-69, 2011.

[29] C. Wang, F. Mueller, C. Engleman and S. L. Scott, "Proactive Process-Level Live Migration in HPC Environments," in *2008 ACM/IEEE conference on Supercomputing*, New Mexico, 2008.

[30] Y. Dai, Y. Xiang and G. Zhang, "Self-healing and Hybrid Diagnosis in cloud Computing," in *International conference on CloudCom*, 2009.

[31] S. Sidiroglou, O. Laadan, C. Perez, N. Viennot, J. Nieh and A. D. Keromytis, "ASSURE: Automatic Software Self-healing Using REscue points," in *International Conference on Architectural Support for Programming Languages and Operating Systems (ASPLOS'09)*, Washington DC, 2009.

[32] D. Bruneo, S. Distefano, F. Longo, A. Puliafito and M. Scarpa, "Workload-based software rejuvenation in cloud systems," *IEEE Transactions on Computers*, vol. 62, no. 6, pp. 1072-1085, 2013.

[33] R. Santhosh and T. Ravichandran, "Pre-emptive Scheduling of On-line Real Time Services With Task Migration for Cloud Computing," in *International Conference on Pattern Recognition, Informatics and Mobile Engineering (PRIME)*, 2013.

[34] V. Kaushal and A. Bala, "Autonomic fault tolerance using haproxy in cloud environment," *International Journal of Advanced Engineering Sciences and Technologies*, vol. 7, no. 2, pp. 222-227, 2010.

[35] "Docker: Build, Ship and Run Applications Anywhere," [Online]. Available: http://docs.docker.com/. [Accessed 2015].

[36] "Nginx: Load Balancer," [Online]. Available: wiki.nginx.org/Main. [Accessed 2015].

[37] "Digital Ocean, Inc.(US), master-master replication," [Online]. Available: http://www.digitalocean.com/. [Accessed 2015].

[38] "OpenNebula, —Opennebula.org: The open source toolkit for cloud computing," [Online]. Available: http://opennebula.org. [Accessed 2015].